Praise for *Sound Spirit*

*"Don Campbell reflects on the profound and meaningful
impact of music in our evolving world community. **Sound Spirit**
is written in such a wise and compelling manner that I will
ponder the musical messages for years to come."*

— **Charles Eagle, Ph.D.**, professor emeritus of music therapy

*"**Sound Spirit** will expand your perspective and appreciation of the role
of sound in spiritual development. Don is an itinerant musical preacher
and peripatetic teacher who helps us transcend language limitations
and cultural differences so we can establish our own sound faith."*

— **Dr. Arthur Harvey**, director, Music for Health Services

*"There is purity and serenity in the vast knowledge that comes
from a life of grist, grace, and revelation in Don Campbell's lifelong,
all-consuming pursuit of the Deep Vibrational Self. **Sound Spirit**
is an offering that will serve the longing ears and hearts of many
who are ready to listen to their own personal calling."*

— **Chloë Goodchild**, founder of the Naked Voice Foundation

*"**Sound Spirit** is one of the most important books
written to help us discover the revelation of music
and spirituality. It is destined to be significant."*

— **Dr. Marilyn Rossner**, cofounder,
the International Institute of Integral Human Sciences

D0731703

Sound SPIRIT

Pathway to Faith

DON CAMPBELL

HAY HOUSE, INC.
Carlsbad, California • New York City
London • Sydney • Johannesburg
Vancouver • Hong Kong • New Delhi

Dedicated to Bess Hieronymus, who devoted her life to the spirit of music.

Contents

I Am
MUSIC

I am music, most ancient of the arts. I am more than ancient; I am eternal, I am spirit. Even before life began upon this earth, I was here—in the winds and the waves. When the first trees and flowers and grasses appeared, I was among them. And when humanity came, I at once became the most delicate, subtle, and powerful medium for the expression of emotions.

In all ages, I have inspired people with hope, kindled their love, given a voice to their joys, cheered them on to valorous deeds, and soothed them in times of despair. I have played a great part in the drama of life, whose end and purpose is the complete perfection of human nature. Through my influence, humanity has been uplifted, sweetened, and refined. With the aid of human beings, I have become a Fine Art. I have a myriad of voices and instruments.

I am in the hearts of all and on their tongues, in all lands among all peoples; the ignorant and unlettered know me no less than the rich and the learned. For I speak to all in a language that everyone can feel. Even the deaf hear me if they but listen to the voices of their own souls. I am the food of love. I have taught people gentleness and peace, and I have led them onward to heroic deeds. I am comfort for the lonely, and I harmonize the discord of crowds. I am spirit. *I AM MUSIC.*

— **Anonymous**

Foreword

The search for meaning lies at the heart of most religious traditions. Don Campbell has been on a lifelong journey of meaning searching and meaning making, exploring the dynamic of sound and music in human life. As a priest and pastor for nearly four decades, I've been privileged to both witness and participate in his search for and enunciation of meanings.

We have explored the intonation of chants, the rhythms of tribal drumming, and the nuances of dance and movement to sound. Sitting in on symphonies and recitals, we've both experienced the soaring delights of virtuosity and technical acumen as well as the subtle subtexts of musical structure. But he has never lost the sheer wonder of the creation of music and its incipient messages of hope and passion, courage and sorrow, or despair and dread. Implicit in these architectures of sound is the ongoing attempt to make meaning and speak of it clearly and without creed, dogma, or belief system. It's perhaps this crosscutting exploration of soundings that makes Don's work both a theological expedition and a philosophical adventure enabling the journey of meaning making to be accessed by all.

The world is constantly searching for meaning, and Don's exploration into the soundings of the ages adds a great deal to our canon of experience. His words have directed me to a deeper appreciation for—and acceptance of—daily musical phenomenon as explorations into faith and community. Sitting in the midst of a chanting congregation in a township in southern Africa as the rhythm guide led us to the ecstatic expectation of the reading and preaching of the holy word, I remembered Don's documented evidence of the role of rhythm in raising consciousness. My expectation for and receptivity of the "holy" was elevated and enhanced in the moment.

Watching the ecstatic rhythm maker raised up by the sheer power of the chant and drumming on hymnbooks, I found that I, too, was newly opened to receive the holy word. Was it the thrumming of the women or the stomping feet of the men that created the sacred space to hear? I know not. That it preached volumes and lifted me to recognizing implicit meanings, I cannot deny.

Don's observations and syntheses bear witness to the fact that music and sound are essential precursors to theology and metaphysics—to helping humankind articulate the meaning of meaning itself. The sound and the fury generated by theological disputes of organized religion can be mitigated by tones and rhythms that can massage the soul, lead to visions of paradise, or warn us of the hell to come.

If you're a searcher for meaning or one charged by the community to articulate or enunciate value, this volume may give you a glimpse or remind you of a poignant memory of the value of sound in informing your faith and experience. Without dogma or creed, Don's current exploration reveals a larger vision of our experience than we perhaps are ready to consider.

But consider this: Some years ago, I stumbled across Bruce Chatwin's timeless volume *The Songlines,* describing the notion of song among the aboriginal people of Australia. He tells how each person has a melody that guides them to their unique songline, which is a grid covering the world. Simply, once you've found your song and songline, you can't ever be lost.

Over the past 26 years, I've worked closely with those living and dying from the effects of HIV and AIDS. Early on when there was no treatment, the focus was on the need for reaching deeply into the souls and hearts of the affected to find the keys of healing and hope. I recall that one evening at a religious service, I challenged the gathering with the question prompted by Chatwin's *The Songlines:* "So what is your song? Which song informs you of who you are?"

In the pregnant silence that followed, a voice burst forth from the rear of the church with this lyric: "Jesus loves me, this I know, for the Bible tells me so . . ." Whereupon the whole group burst into song, singing this sacred lullaby of identity and ownership, pouring out healing balm upon us all. Was there a transformation that night? Absolutely. I never imagined again that those living with and dying from AIDS were far from hope and solace. We weren't abandoned in the midst of the disease! This was *my* healing, which has informed me daily as I've extended this work around the world.

The sounds of faith—from Sufi chants to Hindu mantras—remind us that the music of the spheres is in our bones before it reaches our minds. The gentle tap of the sounding stick in a Buddhist temple enters our hearts before our intellect. Music and sound offer a pathway to find and make meaning before all the words of witness and testimony can be offered. The subtle sound of our mother's perpetual heartbeat, resonating while we're in the womb, provides the assurance and instills in us the hope that the very heart of God will receive and embrace us at last—all this before we can speak.

I recommend this book to you as one who still searches and yearns for wholeness and grace in everyday living. May peace be yours always; but more important, may the sounds and rhythms of life pulse in you, lifting you to renewal.

— **the Reverend Ted Karpf**,
canon, Washington National Cathedral
officer, World Health Organization

Introduction
A CALL TO FAITH

Faith. Hope. Belief. Devotion.

My exploration into consciousness and faith began more than 30 years ago when I met my lifelong spiritual advisor in Jerusalem. As an Anglican priest, he'd lived in and created an ashram in India and was a key participant in establishing dialogue between Muslims, Christians, and Jews. He held weekly meditations on Hindu scripture and served Mass at Saint Anne's chapel in the ancient walls of the holy city. He took me to Sabbath prayer services in synagogues and would stop in his tracks when he heard the daily call to prayer from the towers in the eastern part of the city. Murray Rogers deepened my life, my ability to listen, and my faith. But to sustain it, he said, I needed to become a spiritual archeologist by using my musical tools—only then could I excavate the layers of spirit within many faiths.

Nearly every year, I've reflected on some of the primary questions he asked me:

- What spirit of belief has been constant in your life?

- When did you have great moments of enlighten-ment and inspiration?

- When did you question your beliefs and those of your family and friends?

- What have been the steadfast, unwavering ways for you to feel inspired for most of your life?

- What phases have you been through to find growth and maturity in your faith?

- What kind of startling event has happened to you to awaken the deep concerns of mortality?

These are the questions that continually shape the decisions and actions I've taken in my life. Every decade has challenged me through death, illness, and the human relations that take place in work, love, and music making.

Hunters, fishermen, mothers, priests, prisoners, and composers alike bring the depths of their souls' expression into song, dance, and ritual. From a "High Church" liturgy of bells and incense to the chants and prayers of pilgrims, the voice releases the pain and pleasure of the human spirit and questions God, life, and faith. From praise to curse, we've captured the resonance of the times through music.

"Amazing Grace," "Nobody Knows the Trouble I've Seen," and "I Believe" all express the angst of hope, trial, and faith. As we listen to music, we can feel renewal, refreshment, and that inner release of pain or love that can move us ever so slightly from blues to bliss.

This book is about the sounds of spirit that help us deepen our faith. From ancient chants to folk songs and dance, the power of music instantly connects us with the past, present, and future. We can feel empathy toward slaves and prisoners and be inspired to bring harmony to those around us. We can tap into the great pool of inspiration that has touched mystics and musicians throughout the ages by listening to the remarkable recordings made available over the past few decades. We can dance with the African shamans, the Haitian Christians, and the Native Americans. Our hearts are intrigued with the chanting monks from Tibet, calmed by the Benedictine sisters, and ever inspired by the gospel songs of Mahalia Jackson.

In this book of short essays, the nature of sound and spirit will be explored through song, rhythm, melody, and mood, with the simple goal of reminding us how easy it is to let music be an instrument of faith. These sounds are here to keep us human, remind us of the heavens, and sometimes transport us there. Simple hymns or chants can improve our prayer life; deep listening can reward us with unfettered consciousness, which isn't weighed down by mental materialism. As we look for balance, harmony, and peace in the world, music is an ever-available tool that can transport us to a better place. Whether you're agnostic, Christian, Jewish, Muslim, Hindu, or atheist, the negative will hold you back from living your potential.

"Vibration is the center of all life. We are most alive when we sing together with a magnetic fire," says Alice Parker, composer and conductor. To bring our harmonious spirit into action—alone, together, and with our prayer-filled intentions—we can sound our spirits. I believe that when we transcend the verbal debates of politics, religion, and belief, we can find "active harmony" in this world.

Your spirit is ever alive and awake to inspire you, so let it dance and rejoice, and allow it to be a better listener. Release the left-brain consciousness, and let music in every corner of your mind begin to sing.

— **Don Campbell**
Boulder, Colorado

We are our grandmothers' prayers.
And we are our grandfathers' dreamings.
We are the breath of our ancestors.
We are the Spirit of God.

— YSAYE BARNWELL

CHAPTER ONE

Creating a
SOUND SPIRIT

It's timely that I begin to write more intimately about my relationship with music since my baby-boomer curiosity and exploration of faith have now become primary in the way I approach sound. So much of my professional life has been based on bringing music's healthy powers to our world. My books on music, health, education, and acoustics have always been supported by my own strong faith, which is grounded in sound. Having a family who sang around the piano was my foundation; and I was taken to a church that worshipped through the essentials of great congregational singing, choral masterpieces, and wonderful organ music. The transformation that took place every time I was "inside music" as a child is still the basic inspiration for my work and daily life.

Now, after traveling and studying in 45 countries and living for extended periods in Asia and Europe, I sense that the thread connecting sound to spirit is beyond art and entertainment. Music's power can be raw, startling, and empowering. It need not be just calm and complacent to soothe us; it can dig much deeper to our soul's source of faith and inspiration.

As a young student, the statement "Music is a container; it's an envelope that delivers the spirit" perplexed me. I was busy learning the essentials: notes, techniques, scales, and phrasing. Yet I could sometimes feel "spirit" in a presentation, almost as if the performer or conductor uttered some kind of magical invocation. Why did I sometimes feel spirit when I played or accompanied a choir, yet at other times I felt mechanical or distant from the music? Was this special moment just an emotion, a chemical reaction in my brain, or was it something outside normal consciousness? Maybe there's no answer to this kind of subjective question.

Nothing I write will necessarily make a radical shift in your perception or sensations, but perhaps the music on the accompanying CD will awaken that part of you that resonates to a spiritual state. Each piece may trigger a difference response. The first two selections have text that can focus the mind, while the remaining three don't awaken the verbal part of the brain and may be more inspiring or meditative for you.

Take a moment to recall musical experiences that lifted you to an expanded awareness. Reflect on your most profound spiritual moments and notice if there was music or supreme silence at those times.

Spirit

One of the most important aspects of spirit is its relation to breath and wind—in fact, many languages use the same word for *spirit* and *breath*. There's the constant power in life of breathing in and out. The basic definition of *spirit* from French and Latin means "to blow," and we use the term to imply courage, vigor, and the life force. It can reflect that which holds the essence, the supernatural and mystical consciousness. From divine animations to alcoholic solutions, "spirits" abound.

Spirit is greater than an individual; it's tangible whether seen or unseen, heard or unheard. It's commonly referred to as "the source out of which all things are created"—for example, when God hovered above the waters and the earth. It brings order out of chaos; it has potential. It connects us with others who have an intuitive knowing about the mystical, the religious, and the invisible.

Spirit brings us to a state of wonder and can scare, spook, or soothe us. It's truly about "otherness." The word covers the gamut of definitions with a meaning that seems ineffable at times.

VENI, CREATOR SPIRITUS

Come Creator, Spirit blessed,
and in our souls take up Thy rest;
come with Thy grace and heavenly aid
to fill the hearts which Thou hast made.

— LATIN HYMN

Music is quite the historical handmaiden of Spirit. The primitive utterances of grief, celebration, and invocation all use the breath and voice to call down, call up, and recall episodes of connection. Every culture, religion, and society uses rhythm, song, and chant to "incarnate" or "make manifest" a reality. European soccer matches are a grand chorus of rhythmic prayers and chants for enhancing the spirit of a chosen team. Balinese choirs exorcise the evil spirits and call upon the good ones.

One of my Haitian friends believes that "all night drumming can be heard throughout the universe and gets the attention of the invisible ones." While living in Port-au-Prince for six months, I worked as a volunteer in a children's tuberculosis hospital and played the fine organ at the cathedral. One of my Haitian friends took me to evening Christian-voodoo prayer meetings where I witnessed trance dances in which the spirits seemed to take over the participants during drumming and chanting. At times, there was ecstasy and bliss expressed in the movements; at other points, pain, stress, and panic overtook them. They seemed possessed and out of their rational minds. Sometimes there were reactions similar to Pentecostal prayer meetings with exorcisms and instant healing. I was emotionally affected by these powerful experiences—and somewhat relieved to return to the Episcopal cathedral, where tears of joy were coming from the eyes of my dancing choir.

Music as a gateway to spirit is undeniably an ancient and worldwide phenomenon. Whether we look at vast experiences that are transformational, transcendent, or "magic," music is a bridge from one level of awareness to the next. From one brain state to another, the altered breath, along with spirit, opens our perceptions and sensations to both the hallowed and the haunted.

The Museum of Spirit and Music

How often do we visit a museum and discover a "spirit being" trapped in an "art object"? I think of myself as intuitive at times, although not particularly psychic. Yet on dozens of occasions, I've looked at a room of sacred objects such as icons, figures, sculptures, or carvings and seen vibrations, as if they were singing a tone or making sounds. Some museums display such forms by jamming them together like knickknacks in a crowded market stall, while others give them an honorable environment with plenty of air, space, and fine lighting.

There exists just such a special place to view and experience amazing sacred objects at a museum that opened in Paris in 2006, which holds some of the most unique collection of indigenous power beings on Earth. This institution awakens us to new ways to look, listen, and deepen our experiences with *les objets spirituels.*[The Musée du Quai Branly specializes in the master crafts and spirituality of African, Asian, American, and Oceanian art. Most of the pieces were created for religious or ceremonial purposes.]

This place is unlike any other in the world. A widely traveled public with constant access to television and the Internet arrives at the doors with an intuitive and practical knowledge, as well as an appetite for more than bones and pottery. They want to know about the psycho-spiritual energy behind the creation of a ritual object.

In a way, the Musée du Quai Branly is theater. It moves us, dances with us, and enchants us into the living mythologies of world culture. As a large, 560-foot-long, abstract ship of a museum, it stands on massive columns in a growing arboretum. Thirty multicolored, boxlike rooms radiate out from the sides as viewers from within can glimpse the Eiffel Tower just a block away or the banks of the nearby Seine.

From the amazing garden of 15,000 plants on the ground level, visitors begin to ascend a spiral ramp around a glass wall protecting hundreds of magical musical instruments from every corner of the globe. It's a singing tower of a sacred, shamanic Babel. The ramp leads into a leather-clad grand gallery, where more than 4,000 decorative or sacred art pieces are displayed as part of the 300,000-piece collection, which is divided into works from four distinct geographical areas.

The power of the museum lies in its display of fascinating invocations, songs, and dances. Each of the little box rooms protrudes from the museum; some have four walls of ritualistic cinema, while others contain fine ethnographic and decorative art. After a half-hour of meandering through the dimly lit open hall, the power of these ritual objects begins to take hold of the viewer's unconscious and intuitive reactions to the visual and auditory powers of spirit and art.

Along many of the leather walls are ledges where we can sit in front of small video screens that show sacred rites, complete with narration in English, German, Japanese, or Spanish. We can touch the screen and navigate to footage of a birthing ceremony or a funeral, hear crop songs, or witness the weddings or coming-of-age rituals from a village near where the sacred objects were found. The Sound Spirit is evident everywhere, yet it never overpowers the space—except in some of the small, boxed rooms that extend from the main gallery and feature art, music, or special videos of sacred rites. Never has there been such a worldwide representation of spirit and ritual that can be viewed through a keyhole with our own sense of timing, understanding, and reverence.

Throughout the museum, dozens of languages are sounding. Prayers, drums, chants, and rituals are all alive with style.

We aren't intruding, except in the sense that these grand *objets rituels* have been taken from their home people. Still, these objects are honored here, and with the ears of our hearts, we can feel their beauty and inspiration.

Spirit Music

From the chants of each society and religion, we can learn how these groups heal, soothe, and save. From the dances, we can learn how they move, love, and fight. Spirit is at work and ever ready to transform the experience of common life into either a more introverted reflection or an outward expression of that experience; it moves us and sings us.

People have an insatiable appetite to praise creation and plead with the saints and spirits for better health in this world and the next. The songs and chants of the most conservative Hindus, Christians, or Muslims constantly appeal to the Great One and Its intermediaries for help and special blessings. Even the most radical cheerleaders of gospel music or African drumming call down the Holy Spirit to cast out evil.

Songs of the spirit assist the dying process as well as the marriage ceremony and address the many ills of mind and body. Whether formal or informal, improvised or clinical, music is the constant expression of prayer and empowerment for metropolitan, rural, and solitary supplications.

Ancient and mystical folklore still exists alongside our postmodern age of science and organized religion. Music, sound therapy, and music medicine give some attention to the long lineage of spirit sounds. During their most effective procedures, there's a physical and mental shift.

The familiar story of David playing his lyre to cast out the evil spirits from Saul describes a form of musical exorcism. This isn't as peculiar as it might seem; in mental-health-care facilities throughout the world, music therapists play the harp and guitar to quiet delirium and states of panic. This beneficial effect can also create another reaction, however—one that releases fury. If the evil spirit isn't pacified, it's enraged. It may also be in a state of catharsis when the psycho-physical explosion releases the pain and disorder; a state of calm, quiet, and peace follows.

To open the doors of Spirit with sound is not only peaceful and beautiful, it can be terrifically purging. Some newer faiths tend to ignore harmful energy with uplifting, positive music and prayer, while older and traditional faiths may cling to sin and the fear of negative spirits. Music and hymns can invite a higher, clearer, and more harmonic state of mind and body. Other songs can overtly accent the destructive state of humanity.

My goal in this book isn't to shift or defend any particular faith (or absence thereof), but to enhance your sense of connection to the unseen through music. The current interfaith dialogue and scientific debate allows the real spiritual archeologist to survey the emotions, brain response, and deep sensing that can challenge your faith. Through profound listening and meditation with sound, you can begin to navigate these dilemmas of the conscious mind.

My exploration toward the deepest nature of consciousness is through voice, sound, music, and focused intention. By tone, melody, text, or drumbeat, auditory stimuli organize the brain and body for an experience through which we connect with the unseen.

The will to manifest, to express, and to live is basic to the Spirit. This is the breath of life, the impetus to grow. Our body, emotions, and minds may not always be in harmony, but together they create the drive to express and communicate. Sound, music, the rhythm of speech, and the repetition of auditory patterns set the foundation of our understanding of the world around us.

Music was alive in more spiritual ways 100 years ago than it is today. Recordings in all their forms of digital and analogue delivery give more sonic stimulation to children than any of our ancestors could imagine, but it isn't the same as hearing or making live music or beautiful tones. We spend more time filtering out unwanted noise around us than actually listening to great sound. Ubiquitous headphones, computers, cell phones, air conditioners, heaters, and automobiles create so much spiritless energy that we have to completely reformat our minds and bodies to prepare to receive the magical spirit from music.

LISTEN

The power and spirit of this book is in the music on the enclosed CD. Use it for focus listening, one track per chapter.

Spirit Houses

Spirit House

How I love to walk the paths of Bali, the forests of Japan, and the streets of Thailand where there are little spirit houses in surprising places. A few flower petals, a piece of fruit, or a stick of incense often mark these little structures after morning and evening devotions. These shrines serve many purposes: to bring blessings to the day, to nurture the spirits of the earth, to protect the surrounding area, and at times to honor ancestors. Special houses in the countryside are dedicated to protect and nurture the seasonal harvest. The daily reminder and remembrance of the unseen bring prayers and chants to mind; yet other than an exceptional menorah, mezuzah, or cross, we have few visual places to remind us of spirit in North America.

I remember speaking to one of my Balinese friends who said that spirits would run away from electronics. He mentioned how fans and televisions made them uncomfortable, invading the places they'd always lived. Our ancient connections can get put on "hold" in this fast-paced world, where spirits flee the gadgets with which we surround ourselves. The onslaught of cell phones, MP3 players and personal computers would destroy the world that's seen from my friend's perspective.

Whether or not you believe in the higher realms, you can acknowledge that the electronic "invisibles" have invaded our world and cluttered our minds. Once you tune in, you'll be amazed by how your life is filled with subtle sounds and energy. Notice the "hot spots" in your home. Do you have a room to sleep in that's truly quiet, without the sounds of a computer, a clock, or traffic? Is there a nook for reading or meditating that's free of humming appliances or obvious air-conditioning or heaters? Can you go where nature isn't disturbed by automotive or industrial sounds? Survey your world and find quiet, harmonic places to let your spirit, body, and mind rest. Your ears and soul will thank you.

Deities, Demons, Saints, and Ghosts

Humans have always prayed to the unseen for help, comfort, health, and good fortune. For example, Catholic saints provide intercession for millions of believers every day; their powers from the "Other Side" are believed to mediate and bring harmony, well-being, and peace to those who ask for assistance.

I'm not sure the Vatican would approve of all the popular additions to the powers of the musical saints, but they may be useful for combatting stage fright:

- St. Cecilia, patron saint of musicians, musical-instrument makers, and singers

- St. Genesius, patron saint of musicians, dancers, epilepsy, and lawyers

- St. Dunstan, patron saint of musicians, sword smiths, and lighthouse keepers

- St. Gregory, patron saint of musicians, choirboys, and plague

- St. Jude, patron saint of banjo players, hopeless cases, and those in need

- St. Julian, patron saint of fiddlers and travelers

Gods and goddesses have been assigned to music and the arts in nearly all cultures: Saraswati in India (along with hundreds of lesser-known deities), Apollo and Orpheus in Greece, Bes in Egypt, Ama no Uzume no Mikoto in Japan, and Lan Ts'ai-Ho in China. The great pantheon of musical patrons found in myth and legend provides us with numerous invocations, incantations, and hymns to soothe beasts, breasts, and battlefields.

As abstract and distant as these powers seem to our modern minds, the practice of using sound as a healing modality—in both ancient and modern styles—continues to drive investigation into the relationship between theology, psychiatry, shamanism, medicine, and music.

For a decade, ethnomusicologist Pat Moffitt Cook, Ph.D., investigated the role of ghosts in the healing process in a north Indian village. She found nearly 25 different kinds of beings that could attach themselves to members of the community. These disincarnates usually wanted to cause pain, mental disorders, and sometimes death. The strongest were demons and had powers to completely take over a victim's body and spirit. Most of the ghosts, however, simply materialized from people who had died but whose spirits remained on Earth.

In Pat's fascinating dissertation from the University of Washington, "Ghost Healer: Music Healing in a North Indian Village," she defines the roles of sound and singing for the healer. The ceremony begins with a devotional song to bring in the benevolent spirit of God. The session continues with tunes designed to give a person's spirit strength and courage before the dynamic battle with the negative ghost. The power of the sonic affirmations and the protection from the devotional and strengthening songs remain ever present as protection after the ceremony.

The range of curative powers from song is staggering to our rational minds. We can hardly believe that such events can be relevant to our urban, cosmopolitan lives and routines. To bring this distant world into a modern context, I recall the story of Irish teacher Brian Keenan who was abducted and taken hostage on his way to school in Beirut in the spring of 1986. Often solitary during his five-year confinement, he recalls in his autobiography, *An Evil Cradling*, the powerful and renewing effect of hearing trancelike rhythms coming from the heating pipes in his cell:

> Music was coming from this pipe. I knew there was no music and yet I heard it. And flowing out melodiously was all the music I had ever loved or half remembered. All at once, all simultaneously playing especially for me. It seems as if I sat alone in a great concert hall in which this music was being played for me alone.

Terrified yet drawn to the powerful spirit within the music, he began to move: "I danced and danced. I was a dancing dervish. I was the master of this music and I danced and danced. I felt myself alive and unfearful."

Without priest, shaman, therapist, or guide, Brian rode the waves of sound, releasing the pain of his suppression and confinement, and unconsciously let music bring him back to life.

❦

Silence may be the best preparation for exploring music and spirit. At the end of each chapter, there will be suggestions for listening. The accompanying CD has five selections, each designed to open your heart, mind, and spirit. Reading or speaking can't do the work of a melody.

Take a moment to reflect on this introduction to sound and spirit and prepare to let music do what it does best.

❦

The spirit that's called forth in sound and music is ever ready to bring awareness to life. Whether it comes through chant, quiet prayers, or even the simplest rhythm, we can be awakened and attuned in a matter of moments. Let's bring spirit into being with the wonderful words and music of Ysaye Barnwell. Born into a musical family, Ysaye has shared her amazing vocal talents with millions through the ensemble Sweet Honey in the Rock.

Listening to the Sound Spirit I

Take a moment to clear your mind of ideas, then read the text of "We Are . . ." Read the lyrics again and then close your eyes and reflect on their meaning.

Play Track 1 and allow the spirit of the music to deepen; stop the music after the track is over. Sit quietly for a few minutes and notice what has happened to the words of the song in your mind and body.

Play the music once again and allow its spirit to become familiar. After it's finished, notice if some of the words and melody have stayed with you. Play them in your mind and enjoy the spirit of the music.

Let's bring Sound and Spirit to life. The wonderful text and music of "We Are . . ." by Ysaye Barnwell express the remembrance of our unity and growth, generation after generation.

WE ARE . . .

For each child that's born, a morning star rises
and sings to the universe who we are.

We are our grandmothers' prayers.
We are our grandfathers' dreamings.
We are the breath of our ancestors.
We are the spirit of God.

We are mothers of courage and fathers of time,
We are daughters of dust and sons of great visions.

We are sisters of mercy and brothers of love,
We are lovers of life and builders of nations,
We're seekers of truth and keepers of faith,
We are makers of peace and the wisdom of ages.

For each child that's born, a morning star rises
And sings to the universe who we are.

We are One.

— MUSIC AND WORDS BY YSAYE BARNWELL
LYRICS PRINTED COURTESY OF BARNWELL'S NOTES PUBLISHING

Will the circle be unbroken
By and by,
by and by?

— ADA HABERSHON

CHAPTER TWO

Sarah's Circle of Song, DANCE, AND SERVICE

The circle of sound and spirit holds us, dances us, and awaits us to call out its powers. Being peacefully embraced by the seen or unseen has been basic to human faith from the beginning of recorded time. The soothing balm of energy generated through prayer and meditation has always been a fundamental pathway toward belief in the natural and supernatural. The loving arms of parents and partners hold the "ahs" of safety that establish the core of love, and the beauty of the earth around us inspires praise and adoration.

From campfire songs to dances of universal peace to groups of carolers, music ignites that glorious sense of oneness and harmony. To be a part of tunes that are created from all directions has an aesthetic and spiritual appeal. At concerts and spiritual settings around the world, it's common to hear warmth in the notes as they echo in the space, creating a vibrant acoustical effect that can be transcendent. In early churches, temples, or rectangular Greek halls, the resonance of the atmosphere created a reverberation for five or six seconds. The bouncing sonic waves create an awareness that sound is alive in an extended moment. Time and space are amplified, and it's said that "spirit can live easier in sound when it can dance with itself."

One of the most inspiring "surround sound" experiences of vocal music came into being in the 1840s. The foursquare seating arrangements of early American Sacred Harps can still be seen and heard all over the country. When voices began to come together to sing hymns comprised of notes shaped of little diamonds and circles in a book called a "harp," sopranos sat across from the low basses; and tenors, who held the power of the melody, sat across from the altos. The high energy of voices singing "Amazing Grace" or "Blow Ye the Trumpets, Blow" creates a thrilling effect of poetry and music.

✿

"I live my life in widening circles that reach
out across the world. I may not ever complete
the last one, but I give myself to it."

— Rainer Maria Rilke

In Africa, there are endless variations on the circle song and dance. In South Africa, I recall an amazing Zulu song about friendship and the spirit of trust. "Vulani Ringi Ring" left me with a lifelong impression when I heard it sung and saw it danced at a small school in Alexandria, near Johannesburg. Ladysmith Black Mambazo later made this song popular as they sang of social justice and hope of well-being.

Indigenous people often use the circle as a way to bring down the spirits from above, to capture the essence of an animal, or to call up the wisdom of the earth. Beaver Chief, a powerful spiritual leader and member of the Lummi Nation, a Native American tribe, performs authentic traditional sacred healing circle songs and chants of the northwest-coast Salish people. He speaks of this circle music: "Our old people told us of a time when we would be able to bring out the teachings in 'a good way' and all the people would be ready to hear the teachings of our way of life."

Visionaries, mystics, and prophets have long told us to "listen up, tune in, the time has nearly arrived." Their suggestions may prompt us to be more attentive to the ecological balance of our physical world and spiritual lives. As we begin to differentiate between the "urgent now" and the "peaceful eternal now," we can develop an attentiveness to the next step in balancing the inner and outer worlds.

Around the World in Sound

Between 1975 and 1977, I took trips around the world, starting in Japan where I worked. I spent those summers stopping in areas where I could hear unusual and new music to feed my questing spirit. I visited India and heard much from the heritage of their sacred, sonic cosmos. Danced, sung, and performed on a variety of instruments, this was obviously the country of the Bhagavad Gita, the Hindu sacred book; the title translates as "song of the blessed one" or song of spirit.

As I flew eastward from India, the plane stopped in Dubai and Beirut. At the first city, I was joined by a woman draped from head to toe in a long, black burka. Although the style of this garment was quite different from a nun's habit, I could not help but think of the sisters at Mount Sacred Heart where I went to first grade. I spent the next hour wondering about the heat and the probable discomfort of my seatmate.

A bit later, I asked her if she wanted something to drink, and she answered positively in a refined British accent. We began a wonderful discussion on her work as a doctor and my life as a musician. Being quite ignorant of Muslim traditions, I barely knew how to form a good question; but I'd been in dozens of mosques in Turkey, India, Palestine, Jerusalem, and Malaysia, so I had some intuitive knowledge. We didn't start out by discussing our faiths, however. We just carried on an informal conversation.

She asked me about my music, which had focused around my being an organist, church-choir director, writer, and teacher. She said that they didn't have organs, anthems, or instruments in her places of worship, although she'd visited many cathedrals in England when she was a student and found the music quite interesting. Somehow I managed to ask, most inappropriately, "Don't you think Islam would be spiritually more interesting if they played instruments and had beautiful songs for your services?"

This was truly a moment of embarrassment as I remembered before I even finished the question that there's beautiful chanting and wonderful instrumental music in the Sufi tradition. She said something softly in Arabic and then added, "Because my head, body, and mouth are covered in black, doesn't mean my mind and spirit are covered with ignorance. God is One." I was stunned by my lack of mindfulness and consideration, and I didn't speak to her again, nor she to me.

After a few hours of silence, we landed in Beirut. Before we left the plane, my seatmate turned and gave me a loving wave and said what sounded like some very kind words in Arabic. I never knew just what she told me, but that experience profoundly altered the way I thought about music and its sacredness around the world.

Decades later, I read a poem by Rumi, the great Sufi mystic, and was reminded of that airborne conversation. The verses were about the crying sound made by a reed cut from its family and root, and how it understood the pain of anyone leaving home. As the reed was taken to gatherings, it would be blown upon and people would laugh and grieve, commenting on how beautiful and expressive it was. No one ever heard the secret pain in the notes: "No ears for that. Sound flowing out of spirit, spirit up from the body." The flute made from the reed was empty. It just allowed the vibration of love to flow; it was a simple vessel who missed home.

As I continued my trip from Beirut, I stopped in Turkey to hear the mystical sounds of Sufi instruments playing for spinning spiritual dancers, the dervishes. Reciting the love songs to God written by Rumi, they were transported into ecstasy, and I was stunned with embodied attention. The dance and music took me out of my travel trance and whirled me into consciousness. The longing, pathos, and joy of being held by sound, spinning, and poetry deeply imprinted my heart. It reminded me, oddly enough, of the American Shakers, who danced and sang for hours with the most reverent of hearts. It recalled the most simple motion within Rudolf Steiner's style of movement, *eurythmy* . . . tone led the movements in both spiritual gesture and intent.

In my final trip around the world from Japan, I took trains and planes through Siberia. Finding remarkable Russian Orthodox churches on the shores of Lake Baikal, I felt there were no Soviet eyes looking on. The low chanting and the devotional candlelit atmosphere were haunting and inspiring. The small wooden structures with unearthly icons of saints and prophets held that strange, yet obvious, state of spirituality even when there was no ritual or chanting.

Next, I visited Armenia, where the magical choral music of Komitas instantly covered me with rich spiritual fabrics of sound, finely textured and smooth; and then I traveled to the ancient monastic world of Mount Athos. In the 1970s, there was neither electricity nor automotive transportation on this 30-mile-long peninsula in the northern part of Greece on the Aegean Sea. It was completely dedicated to prayer, reflection, and worship—old monks lived in hovels on the cliff as pure hermits and dozens of monasteries were scattered over the hills and valleys. By hiking unmarked trails, I could sing, chant, and meditate on the slopes of the holy mountain. At about four o'clock one morning at the Great Lavra, the mother monastery, I heard enough *Kyrie Eleisons* ("Lord, Have Mercy") to fill a hundred churches for a thousand years. In the sacred buildings, I could sense an almost tangible quality of being. Whether in these isolated, ancient structures of medieval

Christianity or in a Zen Buddhist temple in a remote forest in Japan, there was a distinct feeling, an energetically subtle incense wafting. It was this invisible sensation that continued my spiritual excavations.

From Greece, I played organs in cathedrals in France and climbed to the belfries of the great bell towers of Belgium to play the carillons—and my heart and ears are still ringing from those experiences. I traveled to Spain to hear the boys' choir at Montserrat, the great shrine and monastery devoted to the Black Madonna. Then I journeyed north to England, where I heard the magnificent cathedral choirs at Winchester, Ely, Wells, York, and Salisbury.

I continued to the northern part of Scotland to the Findhorn community, where I performed as pianist in a concert with two cellists. That recital of the Handel concertos was the most mystical experience I've ever had at the keyboard—spirit played me. It was the closest I've ever been to levitation and exaltation.

The music took place in the meditation room, which in the early years at Findhorn was in a house. Chairs were placed in a semicircle; a few Impressionist paintings adorned the walls. A grand piano, the focal point in the middle of the room, and a candle were all that created the atmosphere in the vibrating, quiet place, similar to what I could feel in some churches and monasteries. This physical presence, a quiet harmony, provided proof of spirit.

❧

I traveled more than 20,000 miles each of those summers, and I became more curious about this world of spirit and sound. I listened to shamans in Siberia, instrumentalists in Bukhara and Alma-Ata (Almaty), and Russian choirs in Kiev. Within the next decade, I heard the spiritual singers of Brazil invoke the Virgin Mary over a span of eight hours and listened to the raspy voices of shamans in the Amazon sing from the trees. Foreign and familiar spirits led my search for the remarkable in sacred music.

How often are all of us just wanting to be home and filled with spirit, allowing our vessel of mind, heart, and body to feel complete?

❧

PRAYER

Heal these nations, their races, their face
To love each other and spirits embrace.
Heal this earth of forests and seas,
That we never misuse its bounty and gleam.
Heal this spirit, this breathing of Light,
That our actions and movements be ever right.
Heal us again and again, forever each breath.
Let spirit sing in every corner of the world.

Amen

Sarah

In all Abrahamic faiths, Sarai is the most interesting woman in early recorded history. She was married to Abraham when her name was changed (by God) to Sarah as she moved with her husband to Canaan. When she was 90 and Abraham was 100, they laughed as they were told (by God) that she would bear a son, Isaac (meaning "God has smiled")—and indeed, she seemed unable to bear her husband a child. So Abraham fathered a son, Ishmael, with her maidservant, an Egyptian woman named Hagar. Years later while traveling, Abraham claimed Sarah to be his sister.

This woman's story is hardly matched by any other in history—it's complex, interesting, and startling. The details are noted in Genesis 17–21 as Sarah's story continues with more challenges and intrigue than any modern author would create.

Matthew Fox, priest, writer, and theologian, states that Sarah has been an important symbolic figure to modern women because of her creativity, joy, birthing, love, community, and laughter. In *A Woman's Journey to God,* Joan Borysenko writes of an even more symbolic role for this character and defines Sarah's circle: "The center of the circle for a woman is her heart, the Inner Light, the intuition, the voice of God. Her journey is one of orienting to the center of the circle so that she can hear the guidance that always comes from within and use it wisely for the greater good. . . . Sarah's Circle is a relational journey in the company of other travelers." It is here that we sing and dance the spirit of unity.

LADY OF THE SEASON'S LAUGHTER

Lady of the season's laughter
In the summer's warmth be near;
When the winter follows after,
Teach our spirits not to fear.
Hold us in your steady mercy, Lady of the turning year.

Mother of the generations
In whose love all life is worth
Everlasting celebrations,
Bring our labors safe to birth.
Hold us in your steady mercy, Lady of the turning year.

Goddess of all times' progression,
Stand with us when we engage
Hands and hearts to end oppression,
Writing history's fairer page.
Hold us in your steady mercy, Lady of the turning year.

— KENDYL GIBBONS

The power of Sarah's symbolic image invites us, male and female, to join hands and hearts to bring harmony to our world. "Sarah's circle" has manifested in dozens of organizations. In 1979, three women in uptown Chicago decided they wanted to help at-risk and homeless women in their community and create a forum for feminist discussion. For nearly three decades, Sarah's Circle volunteers have set the group's mission as providing "daytime supportive services in a welcoming, safe refuge for women who are homeless, or at risk of becoming homeless. We respect each woman and her individuality, and offer her the opportunity to make positive changes in her life. We work toward ending homelessness by providing options, services and advocacy, meeting the needs of the women who come through our doors."

Kathy Ragnar, executive director of Sarah's Circle, describes how a donated piano in the main room of their center is a magnet. Most of the women in their 40s and 50s remember hymns and songs from their childhood; and playing, listening, and singing with the piano makes them feel at home.

Sarah's circles have taken many forms. In Missouri there is a retreat center called Sarah's Circle; in Minnesota and Wisconsin, churches have book clubs; in Massachusetts there's a publisher devoted to spiritual circles; a prayer group is found in Virginia; in California, a sacred-dance group; and there are interfaith gatherings throughout the world that look to the center of a circle for glimpses into the divine and infinite. The Sophia Center at Holy Names University in Oakland, California, has included the dance and song of Sarah's circle in their collection of body prayers. American folksinger Pete Seeger took the familiar African American tune "Jacob's Ladder" and shifted the text to include a familiar yet new verse: "We are dancing Sarah's Circle . . . sister, brothers, all."

Most of the groups I've mentioned have been inspired by this simple song and found their origin in its name. In the coming chapter, we'll explore the difference between the spiritual ladder and circle and how our music can both lift and embrace our lives.

Listening to the Sound Spirit II

This beautiful arrangement prepared by Sound Circle in Boulder, Colorado, brings the familiar tune of "Jacob's Ladder" and Pete Seeger's "Sarah's Circle" into one meditation. As you listen and reflect on the meaning of a spiritual circle, imagine you're in such a formation, moving slowly with many others. Feel the harmony, the resonance, and beauty of community. Then during the text about the ladder, imagine being lifted upward into light.

Each verse allows us to feel the circle, the ladder, or the fulfilled space of energy and peace where we are ever vibrant, resting and are at one.

We are dancing Sarah's Circle
We are dancing Sarah's Circle
We are dancing Sarah's Circle
Sisters, brothers, all

Every round goes deeper, deeper
Every round goes deeper, deeper
Every round goes deeper, deeper
Sisters, brothers, all

We are climbing Jacob's ladder
We are climbing Jacob's ladder
We are climbing Jacob's ladder
Brothers, sisters, all

Every rung goes higher, higher
Every rung goes higher, higher
Every rung goes higher, higher
Brothers, sisters, all

We are dancing Sarah's Circle
We are dancing Sarah's Circle
We are dancing Sarah's Circle
Sisters, brothers, all

Sarah,
Jacob,
Circle,
Ladder,
Brother,
Sister,
Soul

Guide me, Lift me, Deliver me,

O God

To unknown boulevards that need song and dance

Where I can learn to sound "Yes" aloud.

Guide me, Lift me, Deliver me,

O God

To the mysterious closets that need air and light

Where I can make confetti of Joy

*From the stale, molded, and moth-eaten
garbs of dying rituals*

Glide me, Fly me, and sound me up the Ladder of Love.

Amen.

CHAPTER THREE

Jacob's Ladder
OF LIGHT

The well-known tune of "Jacob's Ladder" was sung in the mid-19th century and published in 1905 in a hymn collection called *Joy Bells of Canaan, Burning Bush Songs No. 2.* Its simple melody was taught in an improvisational manner and could easily be adapted to a variety of musical styles for slow, harmonic meditations or lively, fast hymns that invigorated the singers. The repetition of the words made it easy to learn and remember.

The image of a ladder to heaven is common in Western spiritual systems, such as the Freemasons and many of the esoteric schools throughout the world. Even the popular 12-step programs for addiction recovery—as well as various well-being self-help methods—utilize a step-by-step process to integration and harmony.

Jacob was directed by his father, Isaac, to go to a foreign land, find his beloved, and return with a new wife (which is described in Genesis 28). This is what Joseph Campbell called "the hero's journey," which is very much in the tradition of Parsifal, Moses, Buddha, Osiris, and Christ.

On his journey, Jacob dreamed on a pillow of stones. He saw a two-way "interstate" of angels ascending and descending between heaven and earth, delivering messages from the Almighty. It was an archetypal and universal vision of reciprocal communication between our loftiest intelligence and deepest knowing; higher and lower were communing, and the divine mind and earthly body began dialogue through the unconsciousness.

While it's easy to assume that the ladder symbolized the steps we're to take for a heavenly reward, it's also important to note that it showed we can have a relationship with God that isn't a one-way street. Jacob responded to his dream by taking one of his pillow stones, making an altar, and dedicating it as a holy place.

Alchemists have taken Jacob's experience and turned the ladder into a prismatic or rainbow staircase. In medieval times, they even declared that the musical scale was revealed to Jacob, and that melodies, harmonies, and rhythms from heaven could be created by certain combinations of notes.

Light and enlightenment could be experienced by humanity through the tones, and the "music of the spheres" became an interesting topic of speculation.

Our ability to notate and sing the familiar do-re-mi scale is based on the text of a popular ancient hymn, a prayer of St. John. Guido of Arezzo, an 11th-century choirmaster, took the first syllable or letters from this Latin prayer text that invokes the necessity of being able to sing praises on the marvels of all creation upon a harp so that music could help heal those in need. Early Greek, Roman, and Gregorian scales weren't used in our modern fashion, so the introduction of a prototype scale in Guido's interpretation of this prayer became an important standard in music theory that's still in use today.

The prayer text syllables were interpreted by philosophers to help us understand the mystical, musical ladder of tones. On the following page is one of the interpretations of the descending scale from heaven to earth. It is known as "Guido's Hand."

Do	*Dominus*, God Creator
Si (Ti)	*Sidereus*, stars, galaxies, cosmos
La	*Via Lacteus*, the Milky Way
Sol	*Sol*, the Sun
Fa	*Fatum*, destiny, the planets
Mi	*Microcosmos (Micro, Cos)*, the Earth
Re	*Regina Caeli*, Queen of Heaven, the Moon
Do	*Dominus*, God in Humanity

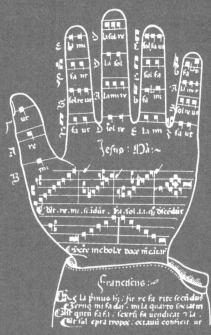

Refining music, architecture, and the arts was part of the magnificent Renaissance quest to see a perfect order for our world and the universe. The early stages of science included investigations into the heavenly designs of mathematics and music. Before the industrial revolution, there was more certainty about the divine order; it was believed that the association between all forms of life was preordained in a perfect pattern. Most New Age cosmology is close to this old worldview, yet it also blends social justice, personal growth, and freedom to create an expansive perspective.

Almost 1,500 years before the Renaissance, Pythagoras began the quest into the relationship between harmony, health, and heaven. The myths and mysteries around his life lead us to question the accuracy of every story, but we can agree that he was the first to separate the powers of music into multiple uses.

Sixth-century Roman philosopher Boethius set out three divisions of music:

- *Musica Instrumentalis* was ordinarily played on the harp and flute, but includes the voice.

- *Musica Humana* was the ever-living music and rhythm produced by the body, even though it was

mostly unheard. It was the song of life created by
the harmonious resonance between the soul and
the body. If it became dissonant, then ill health
would occur in mind and body.

- *Musica Mundana* was created by the universe
  and more commonly referred to as the music of
  the spheres (which I mentioned earlier). This is
  observed as the movement and structure of heavenly and earthly elements as they orbit in the cosmos in harmonic patterns.

A firemist and a planet, a crystal and a cell,
A starfish and a lizard, and caves where ancients dwelt;
A sense of law and beauty, a face turned from the sod—
Some call it evolution and others call it God.

— WILLIAM HERBERT CARRUTH (1924)

The longing to connect heaven and earth, soul and spirit, with the music of the spheres continues. It's a natural quest to strive for a better world here and beyond, although modern society has adapted the golden steps to success for realms of economics and consumerism rather than the holy. Even the need for the ladder as a spiritual image has been challenged by contemporary theologians who say that the image itself is chauvinist, male in nature, and elitist. Some believe that the concept isn't inclusive enough and can't reflect the spirit of nature and the many cultures and beliefs of the world.

Matthew Fox presented the negative consequences of a linear spirituality in his landmark book *A Spirituality Named Compassion*. His work in creation spirituality has presented the need for the more circular, feminine approach to the Divine. Joan Borysenko describes Jacob's ladder and Sarah's circle in her work with women's relationship to spirituality:

> Jacob's Ladder suggests the linear and vertical laws and practices used to communicate with God. As we use foundational moral precepts such as the Golden Rule and the Ten Commandments, we can climb from step to step with specific meditations, prayers, and exercises. This beautiful model serves us all as we develop higher aspects of ourselves.
>
> Sarah's circle is fundamental to relationships and has a spontaneous nature. Women have the intuitive and natural

expression of coexistence. All things and all beings are within this circle with God flowing from the center. This circular relationship allows us to all be in One presence. There is neither beginning nor end. There is no need to climb a ladder; all that is needed is to connect to life within the circle.

The women's journey around this circle is created from daily events in an ordinary life within the family of relatives, friends, and community. In nurturing each other, women worship by creating safe harbors from the trials of life so that people can love more deeply and flower. Mystical unions are born by the rhythms and activities of daily life. Sarah's circle is ever dancing within and around us.

Savina Teubal, Joan Borysenko, Maya Angelou, Jean Houston, Clarissa Pinkola Estés, and Riane Eisler have helped focus attention on women's spiritual rights in Jewish, Christian, Buddhist, and Universalist spiritual circles around the world. The wisdom of the feminine brings balance and the essence of human love to the foreground as both a foundation and a support for humanity.

After spending a quarter century considering these viewpoints of spirituality, I came to realize that there were many ways to think outside the box of the linear ladder as well as to move outside the circle. Related to this is the Freemasons' major visual symbol—the square and compass. The two objects represent the measured and the infinite, the exactness of the linear and the fullness of spirit; they can never have the exact same area or mass. In a way, they can resolve the imperfection of human rationality in regard to the spiritual . . . through faith. Both are real forms whose substance can't be perfectly fit into each other, even though the difference between them appears infinitesimal.

William Gray, a great mystical teacher and Kabbalist, wrote about the necessity of using the "Ladder of Lights" to climb, meditate on, and understand the tree of life, which consists of ten spheres of light connected by ladders or pathways. The universe being a vast circle with no circumference, it was impossible to define, describe, or form. The circle was form-less, and the tree of life symbolized the human body and the whole cosmos.

From the wheels of the chakras in India to Celtic circles, getting "around" the linear spiritual world takes heart- and head-filled practice. It's in this place that music provides both structure and freedom. Rhythms ground us, putting us here in time, while harmony expands us and gives us vast amounts of space. Melody organizes the personality and carries the energy of rhythm and the emotion of harmony. Time and space meet in a vibrational alchemy through music to carry consciousness into spirit.

How to bring both of these ways of faith and action—the ladder and the circle—together was one of the greatest dilemmas of my spiritual life while studying to become an interfaith chaplain. I sensed that each would wither and become weak without the other. The integrative solution is about flow and form, the basic power of music.

Fuji

Three decades ago I met a wonderful sensei (a Buddhist teacher) in Japan who strove to pop me out of my Western, musically trained, rational brain. He insisted that I meditate on Mount Fuji for a week, suggesting that I go there, read about it, and look at its representation in photos and woodblock prints. My first change in awareness came when I realized that I could only meditate on "it" if I were actually sitting at the physical mountain. Otherwise, I was observing, learning information, or contemplating his suggestions.

When I met my teacher again, he asked me what I learned from the exercise. I replied, "There are many empty cans on Fuji. It was hard to empty my mind there." He laughed and said that I'd gotten closer than he thought possible.

He then taught me a visualization exercise that still helps me center and focus mentally and spiritually: "Don-san, close your eyes and imagine Mount Fuji on a clear day outside the window behind me. Now, see yourself sitting on the mountain again. Keep both images and envision a wonderful woodblock print of Fuji hanging on the wall to your right and a brush-stroke painting on your left. Keep all those impressions at the same time as you look down on the sacred mountain from an airplane. Now imagine it in the fog. Can you actually think all of these things at the same time?"

"Yes, nearly," I responded. "I was clear and in control of everything until you asked me to see it from the airplane. I couldn't be in two places at once."

"Go home and meditate more on Mount Fuji," my sensei suggested, "but this time imagine you're a geologist and that the mountain is a big horn you can blow into and make the whole earth sound."

For a few months, my exploration of Fuji took me to every state of mind. Finally, I understood that I needed all the components of visualization, knowledge, and action to provide the full experience and thus become an "empty can" myself. Then I could let it resonate and become a sound. I had to move the wind through the image of my mind, breath, and spirit.

In a way, this is an exercise that has kept me from many polarized or political thoughts about spirituality. A simplified form of general-semantic thinking created a technique quite good for my inquiry into Buddhist meditation. The final suggestion of blowing and making a sound through Fuji's ice-capped crater brought a silent, quiet, and conscious emptiness to life for me—the breath infused the image with vibrancy. The emptiness wasn't stagnant. It was far more awakening than being contemplative. The spirit of Fuji flowed to inspire me to become real . . . the empty mind with full awareness.

The Great Chain of Being

Decades have passed since I started my contemplative process in Japan. Looking for the links of connection between the slippery subjects of spirit, belief, and faith inspires me to delve into this subject while I listen to music.

Only in the last few years have I become aware of the nautical use of the term *Jacob's ladder* as "a rope or chain ladder with rigid rungs." Tightly woven circles of fabric hold the device together, and all the circles are such strong links that they support the weight of body and spirit. Rather than a ladder of flat steps, they're round and create spirals, as the spiritual suggests in some of its verses: "Every rung goes higher, higher."

The Great Chain of Being was a commonplace belief in the cosmic order during the Elizabethan era. "The harmonious concord" of the chain ascended and descended in its own evolutionary theory. For the most up-to-date, psycho-philosophical interpretation of this theory, philosopher Ken Wilber acknowledges that connectedness has been central to spiritual traditions from time immemorial. From shamanism to Taoism to the spectrums of consciousness expressed in the eight *vijanas* of Buddhism, there have always been levels of awareness, knowledge, and initiation.

Most modern and postmodern theories of existence reject all suggestions of a spiritual or metaphysical nature. Yet science is creeping closer and closer to the music of the spheres as it begins to eavesdrop on the great beeping codes, the constant hums and sonic symphonic patterns that are singing to us. As we learn to listen in new ways to our own cosmic surroundings and our human situations, the circles and ladders will begin to dance inward, upward, and beyond anything our divided brains can fathom. It is the ineffable music.

Listening to the Sound Spirit III

From the yearning for human community and connection through the dancing of Sarah's circle to the climbing of Jacob's ladder, we center and ascend to a place of absolute inspiration and peace.

Few composers reach into the ecstasy like Beethoven, who felt the torment of his humanity as well as the bliss of eternity. In this second movement of the "Emperor" piano concerto, just allow yourself to rest and surrender to the spirit of sound. From dancing, climbing, praying, and thinking, just let go and breathe into the great harmony of divinely inspired music.

LISTEN "to the Great wondrous melodious
Spirit which covereth the oneness of us all."

— BOB DYLAN, *WRITINGS AND DRAWINGS*

CHAPTER FOUR

Incline
THINE EAR

"Incline thine ear." This common phrase in prayer and scriptures suggests the need to modify the way we take in spiritual experiences and information. The exploration of the ear's capacity for unearthly receptivity is common to all religions, and techniques in prayer and meditation suggest that silence and breath can create a powerful listening tool for finding the right posture for divine comprehension.

"Listen . . . and incline thine ear to the heart . . ." begins *The Rule of St. Benedict*. Starting in the 6th century, monastics began to reflect on that essential statement as the basis of spiritual growth. To learn the power of silence—its heartbeat—along with sincere outreach is fundamental to all disciplines. Until a century ago, most people were illiterate; reading and writing were exclusively for the spiritual and social lawmakers. The ear was the leader of logic and consciousness, supported by the eye. That has changed rapidly over the course of the last hundred years. We've become so noisy—both visually and acoustically—that we have to work harder to listen to the more subtle aspects of sound.

The ear has often symbolized wisdom. Buddha's long earlobes represent his royal lineage of spiritual listening; Mohammed, Socrates, Homer, and Christ stress the importance of listening. It was a practice, a discipline that would bestow many rewards of wisdom and connection to a more spiritual mind. The Bible mentions listening more than 1,000 times in the Old Testament and more than 400 times in the New Testament.

Spiritual listening is a skill that's cultivated throughout life. The many types of meditation and reflective techniques available today make it possible for the pilgrim of the inner world to find pathways through the mind, body, and emotions to the place of inspired receptivity, peace, and silence.

"This is the essence of Compassionate Listening:
seeing the person next to you as a part of yourself."
— Dennis Kucinich, U.S. congressman

Music affects the brain and body in fundamental ways that science has yet to explain. Its mysterious energy can enchant, energize, heal, and haunt us. Listening is far more than what meets the ear; it's a power that speaks with the spirit and soul, conjuring up memories of distant friends, places, and emotions. Music brings us playfulness, grief, joy, and inspiration. It has drummed out evil spirits, helped stroke patients regain speech and movement, marched us to war, and given us hope for paradise.

The music of the hemispheres is a profound mystery, and deep listening will lead us into the harmony, healing, and exploration of life itself. Do you hear what I hear? Beneath the melodies, rhythms, and emotions, perhaps you do.

We have classes for reading, writing, and speech, yet we take listening for granted. It's the essential sense that gives us the ability to learn language, interpret emotions, and take in complex information about the world around us. *Listening* isn't simply *hearing*. Rather, it's the ability to focus and follow a sound as we simultaneously filter out unnecessary information. Choosing attentiveness in the outer or inner world can be a challenge for anyone, and children with attention deficit disorder (ADD) and attention deficit/hyperactivity disorder (ADHD) often are hypersensitive to sound. Every click, roar, chirp, and rattle magnetizes their attention, if only for a brief second.

A room or restaurant where many people are speaking can create chaos for the ear, mind, and heart. Even the best of listeners feels exhausted after a half hour of roaring cacophony. Yet when there are cheers of joy and enthusiasm at sporting events and the ear isn't challenged to listen, just hearing the changing sounds can charge and invigorate the mind and body for a short period.

The Church of Conscious Harmony

Since I was a child, I've been interested in the music and the feeling I experienced in houses of worship. From the Jewish temples and Catholic churches to the more conservative meeting halls of Quakers and Christian Scientists, I could feel a tangible quality of spirit. Later, in Zen temples in Japan, I felt a similar quality. It was a harmonic silence. I've often wondered if sound and energy lingered in some measurable way in places of worship, perhaps like a form of incense.

A few years ago, a dear friend in Austin, Texas, told me about the Church of Conscious Harmony, where listening was paramount and energy was perceivable. So I visited and sensed what was referred to as "a monastery without walls." Not only are there contemplative music and provocative sermons, but there's also time given for reflection and inner dialogue with divine inspiration. Developed from the Centering Prayer teachings of Father Thomas Keating, this community has developed a family-centered, vibrant, and young following.

When I entered the church, there was soft and mystical piano music setting the atmosphere before a service. It wasn't "New Age" music. It sounded familiar, but nowhere could I place its sound. Later I discovered it was the music of George Ivanovitch Gurdjieff, the Armenian mystic who collaborated with Russian musician Thomas de Hartmann in creating music with titles such as "Holy Affirming" and "Holy Reconciling."

I was embraced in silence, song, chant, and reflection for two hours. The ministers, Barbara and Tim Cook, brought together a spiritual, prayerful centering for the members of this congregation. In a stunning modern sanctuary under a cone-shaped roof, we sat in reflection as Webber's "Pie Jesu" was played sensitively with long spaces of silence between each phrase. The quiet provided a chamber of space where I could re-sing the phrase a couple of times myself in my own inner echo chamber.

What impressed me about those two hours was more than the music and the atmosphere. During the time of the sermon, Tim Cook told about the suicide of a church member a few weeks before and how the previous Sunday everyone had felt profound shock and grief. Now he felt it was important to deepen that experience and asked members of the congregation to share their "wisdom" from this tragedy. Taking microphones from the beams of the church, a few members spoke from deep emotion and reflection. After each one spoke, Tim asked the community to enter silence and reflect on what had been said.

To me, seldom has there been quite so powerful a use of silence and contemplation in a worship setting. Although it's common in transpersonal therapy, I've found it rare as a listening practice used throughout a morning worship service.

This vibrational listening and prayer was so filled with the presence of love and devotion, the sacred spirit of conscious harmony was actualized.

Excavating the Spiritual Ear

The work and research of Alfred A. Tomatis, M.D., (1920–2001) is at the forefront of scientific and spiritual frontiers in the anatomy of listening. He documented and observed the evolution of the ear and its role in human development. From the first signs of the ear in the jellyfish to the complex auditory and vestibular functions of musicians and athletes, he brilliantly observed how this organ coordinates sounds, movement, and balance.

Tomatis's work looks at the ascent of consciousness through the ear's ability to balance the body, perceive the space around the physical self, and focus on meaningful information for both survival and expression. The greatest challenge was to bring the living form to an upright, vertical posture of balance so that language could develop. He even referred to this as "Jacob's struggle" on the ladder of physical and spiritual development.

Without upright posture, the brain couldn't develop the frontal lobes that give attention to the realm of thought, reason, and reflection. Tomatis was clear from both his Roman Catholic background and his scientific quest that becoming an *auditeur* ("listener") would allow us to refine our skills to such a degree that we could travel beyond silence to the "inaudible sounds" of the cosmos. The ear was the human antenna that needed tuning every day through movement, proper listening, and stimulation from the voice.

For Tomatis, listening became more than the reception of sounds of thoughts—it became dialogue with God. Paul Madaule, the director of The Listening Centre in Toronto, says that by exercising the ear and using his "earobic" techniques, the mind, body, and spirit could become stronger and stronger. The proper combination of posture, music, and chanting would create an obvious shift in consciousness. Tomatis referred to this communication with the spiritual world or the cosmos as listening to "the sound of life."

The first time I visited the Tomatis Center in Paris, I was astonished to find a dozen children listening to filtered Mozart on headphones as they drew pictures, worked jigsaw puzzles, and played on swings. In little booths, adults were singing Gregorian chants into microphones with the filtered sound of their voices being reproduced into their ears and the bones of their skulls. Outside on the balcony overlooking the beautiful Parc Monceau sat nuns and businessmen in headphones taking their weekly "Tomatis Cocktail" of Mozart.

From the very first impulse of sound received by the ear in utero, five to six months before birth, up until the last breath of a centenarian, Tomatis was certain of the possibility of staying connected through a perfected state of listening that was balanced, charged, and spiritually attuned.

In his book *Why Mozart?* he stated that his purpose was to "modify the psychological structure [of the mind] in order to free it from the chains that hinder listening." He insisted that humanity was hampering its evolution by concentrating on the egocentric materialism and horizontal wealth of the world. Self-realization was the goal, not ego fulfillment.

Tomatis's research is complex and fascinating. I've written at length on his work, methods, and cosmology in my books *The Mozart Effect* and *Music: Physician for Times to Come*. There are hundreds of centers around the world that have used some aspect of the Tomatis Method in audio-phonology to help children with speech disorders, singers with tuning and vocal challenges, students who are learning foreign languages, and spiritual practitioners who wish to improve their listening skills. The questions that arise from his theories are always being tested and revised as new technologies are developed. He was aptly called "the doctor who listened to the heart of the universe."

In his last book, *Écouter L'Univers*, Tomatis wrote in a most abstract style about sound in the universe from the big bang to Mozart. By using humming, the *"aum"* sound, or some Gregorian chant, the vibration created in the cranial area of the body can be tuned, he believed, to a spiritual resonance. "Chant," he said, "charges the brain when done properly. The soul recovers its essential vibration, its perfect rhythm which belongs to our original state of being."

Learning how to charge the brain with sound is essential to prayer and opening the clear channel of divine communication. To pray without the use of chant or sound is difficult because our thoughts get in the way of a pure state of listening. Tomatis often questioned whether we were listening to our self-created god or the "far away regions where only the heart listens."

As I studied his chant technique in Paris, I knew he was caught between vocal performance and the inner place of pure sonic resonance. He moved between the worlds of structure and posture for the body and flow with the resonant voice. In my most recent book, *Creating Inner Harmony* (Hay House, 2007), I also used many of Tomatis's humming and sounding techniques to open up the inner voice.

Your personal faith may not have a cosmic sound or a complicated prayer life. You might simply understand how to find the "still, quiet voice of peace." Your intuition may know how to differentiate between listening and hearing. No one can judge; we can only point out the wisdom of musicians, cantors, chanters, and others who inspire us to live full, resonant lives. Tomatis was so curious in his quest that clergy, parents, and students alike feel that he was intuitively on the right resonant track of sound realization.

Ear Number Three

A wise old owl lived in an oak
The more he saw, the less he spoke;
The less he spoke, the more he heard—
Why can't we be like that wise old bird?

— Nursery rhyme

Many of us are accustomed to the phrase "seeing with our third eye" as it refers to spiritual insight. *Ear* number three isn't placed in the middle of the forehead, but resides in the bones and skin throughout the body. It's the extended perception of vibration that reaches from the top of the skull to the tip of the toes.

Helen Keller was the expert in third-ear listening. With her hands, she could feel the vibration and its emotion in the face of another. She could put her hand on a Victrola phonograph and sense the patterns of music played through the rhythm, accented beats, and tempo.

Dr. Tomatis emphasized the importance of the bones in the listening process. When he designed the "electronic ear"— a device to filter and enhance frequencies for improving auditory processing—he delivered the sound with headphones that had a special speaker just for bone conduction at the very top of the skull. It's easy to sense the patterns and flow of the music through this instrument, even though it isn't the same as acoustic listening.

The bones in our body are living. Sound travels faster through them than through the air. Hard, yet filled with living liquid, these magical mallets supported by muscle often have listening abilities that are quite different from our normal ears. Audiologists are aware that some children who don't hear well via the air are able to compensate through the conduction in their bones.

If you put your hands on your cheeks, close your eyes, and begin to hum a tone, you'll feel the power of sound in the bones of your face. When you place the palm of your hand on the top of your head, close your eyes, and hum, it's easy to notice the vibration. You can massage your brain from the inside out with the power of your voice. Whether you decide to hum, vocalize an *aum,* or stay on a elongated *Aaah* sound, after a few minutes, you'll notice that your inner mind is calm and peaceful yet refreshed, not groggy.

It's obvious why the power of song and chant is so important to spiritual well-being. The breath, as discussed in Chapter 1, is spirit in many languages. By vibrating and embossing the breath with tone— amplifying it with the intent of prayer, praise, or calmness—you can create a peaceful and clear state of mind. Your inner and outer worlds will be in harmonic phase. You can easily open the doors of quiet perception and in the time afterward sense the "still, small voice within." This may be what so many philosophers and mystics have called listening to "the music of the spheres." It may be the opening to the third ear.

"Hidden harmony is mightier than what is revealed."

— Heraclitus

In Mozart's personal letters, he noted that he'd often see and feel a composition all at once, in a glance. All of the notes were heard simultaneously in his mind. He seldom rewrote his music; it was perfect as he inwardly sensed it. This combination of inner sight and sound created a spiritual impulse for him to compose. Bach improvised and wrote his music, noting at the end, *Soli Deo Gloria*, "to the Glory of God alone."

In contrast, Beethoven was haunted by hearing loss and wrote and rewrote his music with both emotional and physical stress. His remarkable compositions take us to ecstatic heights of spiritual surrender after the storms and mad moments of his agony. "Music is a higher revelation than all wisdom or philosophy," he wrote.

He wrestled with the angels and demons of sound. His doubt, rage, joy, and pain send the listener on the journey of contrast within the human condition. It is as if his ear opened and closed in such a way that he heard the cosmos in one moment and then in the next instant shifted to the anguish of the emotions and body. Beethoven's genius expressed doubt and hope, ecstasy and stress; he was one of the first composers to reflect the entire contrasting spectrum of emotional and spiritual conflict of the human experience.

◦◦◦

Our ears and eyes have quite a job in filtering out all the stimuli around us. The ear takes in and interprets the sound spectrum from 30 to 20,000 vibrations per second when we're young, and this auditory range is limited compared to many animals. Our lives are spent looking and listening through a small keyhole of what's happening in a larger vibrational field. The third eye and ear simply remind us of what's already here around us that we don't immediately sense. One of my spiritual directors told me a definition of God was "the great One Who has a thousand senses. We are just growing into our sixth one. Be patient and we will all be One."

This is poetically expressed in this passage from T. S. Eliot's "Four Quartets."

> *Words move, music moves*
> *Only in time; but that which is only living*
> *Can only die. Words, after speech, reach*
> *Into the silence. Only by the form, the pattern,*
> *Can words or music reach*
> *The stillness, as a Chinese jar still*
> *Moves perpetually in its stillness.*
> *Not the stillness of the violin, with the note lasts,*
> *Not that only, but the co-existence,*
> *Or say that the end precedes the beginning,*
> *And the end and the beginning were always there*
> *Before the beginning and after the end.*
> *And all is always now . . .*

Do You Hear What I Hear?

For classical musicians, ear training is fundamental for basic music education. Learning to listen for intervals between sounds, harmonic sequences, rhythmic patterns, and structural counterpoint is similar to learning the anatomy and physiology of the body. System upon system (harmony, rhythm, and melody), each independent in their own way, still rely upon each other for the overall effect. The instrumentation and interpretation of compositions create endless variants for the performer and listener alike.

Classical-music students seldom have any training in regard to the auditory and vestibular functions in the ear, the brain, and the body. There's hardly ever a suggestion of spiritual listening in our music education. Yet jazz musicians have an uncanny ability to be "inspired." Learning music takes technical skills before interpretation can begin. Only in more esoteric training, such as the Alexander Technique, have musicians observed the importance of the connection between the ear and the body. They may not realize that the left and right ears can be as different in their abilities to perceive sound as the right and left hands are in their functional dominance.

After many years of teaching listening skills, much of what I do today revolves around the audiences of symphony orchestras. Within a couple of hours, many kinds of listening take place while witnessing these artists. Watching the performers, recognizing familiar melodies, following the rhythms, and feeling the emotions are but a few of the ways we experience a living concert. Some of the time our listening style may be focused on the structure of music, its place in history, the events in its composer's life, and even the deep philosophical intent of the music's creation. The symphonic experience also depends on our physical health, how stressed we are, and the comfort of the seats in a concert hall.

No matter what our musical background is, the listening experience varies day by day. We may be so familiar with some pieces that we expect them to result in our favorite performances. Or the composition can be so strange and so distant from our normal listening habits that we may not have a vocabulary to understand it.

These factors all come into play in religious services as well as commercial performances. Listening as a spiritual experience has always been a part of worship. Sometimes it's entertaining, sometimes it's reflective, and often it's prayer. Now drumming and singing circles create a new opportunity for many who want to participate in sacred music making, although there are still challenges to overcome.

When I began my work with educators and health professionals more than 20 years ago, I sensed that my students weren't all hearing the same things. Critics often describe the same performance in such varying ways that it's difficult to believe they were in the same concert hall. Early in my own career as a teacher of students from 60 countries with more than 40 primary languages, it became obvious that auditory information was processed somewhat differently because of the way the individuals actually heard their main language. Music became a bridge for them to learn language, movement, and emotional expression.

We readily accept that the left and right eyes may have different abilities in near and distant perception, as well as in the peripheral spheres; they may perceive color differently and can even be color-blind. Eyes are tested regularly for vision and clarity in various ranges of focus. Being aware of the visual world is called "seeing." We see many things at once, yet we know that focused visual attention is referred to as "looking at" an object.

"Hearing" is the passive ability to perceive sound, while "listening" is the active ability to focus on certain sounds and attend to them. As I mentioned earlier, Tomatis was the pioneer in this research. Still today, after a half century of listening analysis, auditory perception and assessment seldom take into consideration the many dimensions of the ear's role in laterality, spatiality, verticality, expression, language, and musicality.

The ear's relationship with the tenth cranial nerve, also known as the "vagus nerve," sensitizes the larynx that allows us to sing, speak, and make various primal sounds. Bone conduction can be highly sensitive and make it difficult for the listener to concentrate on reading and focusing on speech, because we hear the vibration with our whole body. The skin, the bones, and the mind can reach out as an extended ear. As we lift up our hearts, incline our ears, and embrace the greater harmony around us, there's a connection to the spirit. There's no need to wait for it to speak or inspire us, we can tune in to the inspiration by listening with more than our physical ears.

Pauline Oliveras, composer and author of *Software for People,* proposed 17 ways of listening in her creative essay "Sonic Images." She asks us to listen to all sounds equally and find a place in the mind where there are no thoughts or images as we do so. She helps us explore the depth of sound that exists in our minds. How different is our imaginary sound from the real one? Through exercises and meditations, her techniques and music bring a focused attention to the awakened ear.

Marshall McLuhan, known for the phrase "the medium is the message," also suggests in his influential writings on communication, "I wouldn't have seen it if I hadn't believed it." Can this be true of our spiritual ears? Do we have to have faith in order to receive the great harmony of the spheres or the speech of angels? Perhaps sonic experiences in both extreme silence or cacophony prepare us to find the great divine sounds. Music, tones, prayers, and meditation all dance together in building a bridge for spiritual listening.

Listening to the Sound Spirit IV

Mozart's ear was so attuned to the flow of sound that he once wrote, "I usually don't compose, I just have to find time to write down what I hear." Many great artists are able to enter the flow of sound and just let it come through them—for example, jazz and gospel musicians are ever in the spirit. Indian performers invoke the spirit in music through demanding scales and rhythmic patterns and then become remarkable channels of sound through improvisation. The classical music of northern and southern India insist on rigorous technique and rules as well as complete surrender to the spiritual flow.

In this lovely, slow movement of Piano Concerto no. 26 in D Major, Mozart provides a perfect spiritual pillow of sound for resting the mind and body.

Take a few minutes to prepare for the deep listening of this work. Balance your breath, relax your body, and then allow the music to speak to you. Let your skin, bones, and muscles absorb it.

❧ ꧁ ❧

"Music expresses that which cannot be said and on which it is impossible to be silent."

— VICTOR HUGO

CHAPTER FIVE

The Soul of SOUND

Oh soul, where art thou? Must I call on you? Where do you live? How can I lose you if I don't know where you are?

The words *spirit* and *soul* have become so interchangeable in our day-to-day conversations about spirituality that few people can reliably define them. Spirit is much clearer to us. Yet when we "rock-a my soul," "lift my soul in praise," or fear our soul is being cursed, there's a suggestion that it's a substance or place that resides in the body or mind.

From soul music to soul food, the power of an inner essence in the midst of expression is core to understanding this part of ourselves. The dictionary defines the soul as "an entity which is regarded as being the immortal or spiritual part of a person, and though having no physical or material reality, is credited with the functions of thinking and willing, hence determining all behavior." From the initial "animation of life" to the worlds of deep emotions and feeling, the soul is vital to the self.

Biographies of the Dalai Lama *(The Soul of Tibet)* and Pope John XXIII *(Journey of a Soul)* use the word in a temporal way. Most Hindus and some Buddhists believe in the transmigration of souls, a core of energy that emits the life force from infancy until death, then journeys on to its destiny of higher or lower forms of consciousness and embodiment.

Bertrand Russell, the great 20th-century philosopher, writes: "When I was young we all knew, or thought we knew, that man consists of a soul and a body; that the body is in time and space, but the soul is in time only. Whether the soul survives death was a matter as to which opinions might differ, but that there is a soul was thought to be indubitable."

In Kashmir and India, there are many references to *spanda,* the core vibration and impulse of the universe. It's said to live in the hearts of all individuals and is the first throb, tone, and movement; it creates the "will to be." The Spanda Foundation defines *spanda,* the soul of the universe, as "the original, primordial, subtle vibration that arises from the dynamic interplay of the passive and the creative polarizations of the Absolute, and that by unfolding itself into the energetic process of differentiation bringing forth the whole of creation."

The power of the unheard sound, the unseen light, and the untouchable being is described in many ways throughout spiritual traditions. From the highest point on the tree of life to the whirling spirals of galaxies, the unnameable, we're at a loss for words or concepts for this essence. In Buddhism, Nirvana (the clear state where there is no movement) is reached through a *satori* experience, a blowout of all mental concepts. The old gospel hymn declares, "I've got a home in Gloryland that outshines the sun." Gloryland is found through complete surrender and reaching the top of Jacob's ladder where there's no rung. A wonderful modern hymn sings the goal of Sarah's circle: "Break not the circle of enabling love where people grow, forgiven and forgiving; break not that circle, make it wider still, till it includes, embraces all the living."

Back to Earth

Through the prefrontal lobes of our left and right brains, we can experience such vast concepts as *love, justice,* and *compassion*—words that have flowing boundaries in their definitions. The laws of the ladder and the "here-and-now" sensing in the circle live together in these concepts. Scientists question, debate, and try to define what can and can't be analyzed to perfection. Artists paint, dance, write, and sing about the unity of these differing worlds in expressive and, at times, emotional manners.

Ken Wilber delves into the ultimate questions of being in *The Atman Project*. He looks at the whole biological, psychological, and spiritual universe in a transpersonal way that attempts to open dialogue in this postmodern world. Young Tibetan monks enter into lively debates on the states of being as was done by philosophers in ancient Greece; there's a constant search for the perfect law, the ideal community, and the refined state of mind and being. Carl Jung tackled these questions like an athletic professional on the field of the unconscious in his book *Modern Man in Search of a Soul*. Published in 1933, his questions and insights are still timely even though the pace and population of the world has rapidly accelerated.

The sense of disconnection with a "yonder" God, an inner God, or the community in which we live constantly drives us. The role of healers in this human dilemma has now been taken on by psychologists, psychiatrists, clergy, gurus, and medical scientists. This postmodern state of the world is fragmented and overloaded with sensory input—never has there been a time when there were so many beliefs and doubts. A new flavor is always being added to the spiritual stew and brew; we can blend, season, and serve the fresh produce of inspiration combined with sonic succotash, and a meal of worship begins. We can now "Google for God" and have a wireless connection with the world at large. We can worship online, and perhaps we'll soon be able to have soul implants delivered by Express Mail.

Elaine Stritch, the actress, singer, and entertainer, recently said in her one-person show *At Liberty*, "It almost all happened without me!" Her busy career and her addiction to alcohol ("spirits") kept her from integrating her inner life with the outer activities. No matter our accomplishments, traumas, and fears, the key to a soulful and spiritual life is about entering the harmonic state of "showing up, being real," and becoming more aware and conscious.

Where can we live in the midst of knowledge, intuition, and spirituality? I've been so fortunate to live in Europe and Asia, work in dozens of countries, and observe the many ways spirit and faith are experienced. My core beliefs from my childhood experiences in the Methodist church and my experiences working as a minister of music in many denominations have blended with decades of meditation, which I learned in Asia. My heart was opened during a four-month stay in Israel, and my mind was blown to smithereens by the drumming, chanting, and dancing of my extended times in Haiti.

The miracles with music that I've seen throughout the world still astonish me. Some of my closest friends and family are devoted Christians and Buddhists, while others are truly agnostic and waiting for a sign from above, below, or within. During my two years of interfaith studies, I found how important it was to have core beliefs and essential questions.

The purpose of this book is to amplify your ability to use sound and music as a pathway to greater faith—whatever your faith may be. As the stress of daily doubts recurs in our routine, music, quiet, prayer, and sound can bring that harmony of spirit to your mind and body.

The Great Silence

Silence is the border between the spirit and the body.
Some groups start with silence and it
grows into prayer and listening.
Some meditation groups take silence
as the primary path to enlightenment.
Other groups drum, sing, dance until the senses
are filled, and then leave a place of quiet emptiness.

At the turn of the 20th century, Nobel Prize–winning physiologist Robert Koch predicted that "one day humanity will have to combat noise as we once combated cholera and the plague." With the birth of the recording industry, electricity, the auto industry, and the world of radio and television broadcasting, that increased volume became evident decades ago. With mobile phones, the scourge of invasive ringtones and one-sided conversations has become a constant addition to our soundscape.

From hissy white noise to roaring "pink noise" (another type of auditory pollution), the world has become a dumpster for unwanted sounds. It's ironic that people who are exposed to the loud noises of weaponry, music, or industry develop hearing loss and tinnitus—the damage to the small hairs in the cochlea causes our brains to ring.

When we enter into absolute silence in an anechoic chamber, there's only the slightest movement of airwaves and sound. Used for hearing-analysis testing and in industrial-acoustic settings, these small rooms allow us to hear what's going on in our own inner worlds—and it's surprising to discover that silence is everything except quiet. The heartbeat, breath, and slightest physical movements create sound.

In such a space, there's true isolation from the resonant world. We can feel it in our bodies, on our skin, and our sense of spatial awareness is reduced. After an extended time, inner voices and sounds may become apparent. When there's little light, we're truly in a solitary place of confinement. Nothing seems spiritual in this kind of environment. In contrast, the monks and ascetics who retreat into silence of the mountains, caves, and deserts take the rustling of nature with them.

Having no atmosphere to carry sound waves, the air just a mile above us is quiet—at least to our hearing threshold. The music of the spheres is noisy, but not to our ears. A place of silence is often considered to be one that's under 20 decibels. It has relative peace, quiet, and harmony but isn't necessarily void of wind, breath, or movement.

In music, silence is the minute articulated space between notes. In Benedictine monasteries, the "Great Silence" is the time of rest before a day of work and chanting begins. It's not only about sound's absence; there's also a sense of a mysterious presence. This Great Silence represents an immense nothingness, the great home, our origin.

"For things are not mute: The stillness is full of demands, awaiting a soul to breathe in the mystery that all things exhale in their craving for communion."

— Rabbi Abraham Joshua Heschel

Throughout our lives, we search for a sustainable stability of a spiritual state. With daily affirmations, prayers, and music, we can deepen our connection to the great spirit. Music imprints our hopes and prayers through melody, rhythm, and harmony. Whether we dance, walk, kneel, sit, or recline, the opening for the spiritual conversation can be invoked with the daily routines of listening. It may begin as a type of rush-hour request and develop into a deeper weekend retreat. The right kind of music for your spiritual journey can imprint the mind and body.

Just as we can learn to develop our taste for the subtleties of food or scent, we can develop our sacred connection with patience and joy. Hours of meditation with a low, slow drone in the background can keep the mind attuned and the body calm. Repetition of a chant or hymn while walking can stabilize the mind so that clear listening can begin. Whether you start with a simple prayer or song, a Shaker dance, a sacred word, or a podcast invocation, allow the patterns of sound to fill your heart as your circle of community expands and your journey upward and inward continues.

I am "optimystical" that each of us can find and enhance the sacred connection. By using the powers of music, sound, and silence, we're being spiritually active listeners so that we can stay more centered and sensitive to the beauty, love, and creative energies around us. Jean Houston often says that we have very low bliss tolerance. When we get to a resonant state of consciousness, we run toward some activity that keeps us from feeling full and fulfilled.

Faith, doubt, joy, and sorrow are all our teachers. Yet faith can tune us in to our own potential by listening deeply and seeing the best in others. It's the golden resonance—"listen unto others as you would have them listen to you." Faith is uplifted hope; it's where sound and spirit live.

We can transcend the boundaries of faith and respect what we don't understand through active, compassionate listening. How else can we protect ourselves from the terrorists of the heart and heartlands of this world?

Whether we're following the flow of sacred song and dance or the paths of salvation and enlightenment, we're constantly creating a sound world, a sound spirit, and a sound faith that will guide and inspire us. Listen.

Love: The Vibration of Harmony

There are no words that capture the energy we sense in spiritual states of transformation. From the emotional responses in the brain to the rapturous awakening of the body, our perceptions, dreams, and devotions create individual imprints that have always been the challenge for theologians, mystics, and scientists to define. As the prefrontal lobes of the brain fire during moments of inspiration and our words become symbolic of the great expanse of our awareness, we enter into states where we simply experience the unseen mystery that is God.

May these closing words help bring the spirit of faith and trust into your life. May the vibration of love support and expand your belief. May you dance in circles, deepen your love, and climb to the heights of beauty. May the Great Silence be filled with the Harmony of Love.

Sound Spirit Sing
from the hidden chambers of my Heart
where the Soul Eternal
brings me to Life.

Sound Spirit Dance
from the circle of friends
who connect me with the
Joy and Light of this world.

Sound Spirit Ascend
from the fears and pain
that keeps me from living
in resonance with all I am.

Sound Spirit Rejoice
in the spectrum of the senses
and the power of silence
as Harmony heals our world.

Listening to the Sound Spirit V

We've listened to the inspired music of Ysaye Barnwell, Sound Circle, Beethoven, and Mozart. Now we can enter an extended world of meditation for prayer and divine listening with Crystal Meditation.

Imagine a drop of water, falling into a crystal clear pool that represents your personal spiritual life. Each drop of inspiration, wisdom, and love then reverberates and spreads in circular orbits throughout your inner worlds of emotions, intellect, and sensation.

You can see yourself floating in the atmosphere above the earth or in a boat on a quiet lake. You can allow the music to take you wherever it's safe and comfortable. As the drop of spiritual inspiration comes to you, feel the deep and rich tones of the body embracing and absorbing the energy.

Be still and know that the great spirit is ever present. Let music be your bridge.

∽❧∽

CD
TRACK LIST

1. Ysaye Barnwell, "We Are . . ." from *Stick Around,* Sound Circle, Sue Coffee, director + 3:20

2. "Sarah and Jacob" Improvisation on "We are Climbing Jacob's Ladder," Sound Circle, Sue Coffee, director + 4:25

3. Beethoven, Adagio from Piano Concerto no. 5 in E Flat Major, opus 73. Stefan Vladar, piano; Capella Istropolitana, Barry Wordsworth, conductor * 8:00

4. Mozart, Larghetto from Piano Concerto no. 26 in D Major, K. 537. Jeno Jando, piano; Concentuus Hungarius, Matyas Antal, conductor * 4:02

5. Campbell, "Crystal Meditation," Don Campbell. Excerpt from the album Essence * 18:59

+ Used with permission from Sound Circle
* Music licensed courtesy of Spring Hill Music LLC

Suggested READING

Circle of Song. Kate Marks. Santa Fe, NM: Full Circle Press, 1993.

The Feminine Face of God: The Unfolding of the Sacred in Women. Sherry Ruth Anderson and Patricia Hopkins. New York, NY: Bantam Doubleday Dell Publishing Group, 1992.

Finding Faith: A Self-Discovery Guide for Your Spiritual Quest. Brian D. McLaren. Grand Rapids, MI: Zondervan Publishing, 1999.

"Ghost Healer: Music Healing in a North Indian Village." Patricia Moffitt Cook. Unpublished dissertation. University of Washington, 2005.

The Infinite Harmony: Musical Structures in Science and Theology. Michael Hayes. London: Weidenfeld & Nicolson, 1994.

The Ladder of Lights. William G. Gray. London: Helios Book Service Ltd., 1968.

Music and Soul Making: Toward a New Theory of Music Therapy. Barbara Crowe. Lanham, MD: The Scarecrow Press, Inc., 2004.

Music and Trance: A Theory of the Relations between Music and Possession. Gilbert Rouget. Chicago, IL: The University of Chicago Press, 1985.

The Music of the Spheres: Music, Science, and the Natural Order of the Universe. Jamie James. New York, NY: Grove Press, 1993.

The Roar of Silence: Healing Powers of Breath, Tone & Music. Don G. Campbell. Wheaton, IL: Quest Books, 1989.

Sarah the Priestess: The First Matriarch of Genesis. Savina J. Teubal. Athens, OH: Swallow Press, Ohio University Press, 1984.

Software for People. Pauline Oliveros. Baltimore, MD: Smith Publications, 1984.

A Spirituality Named Compassion: Uniting Mystical Awareness with Social Justice. Matthew Fox. Rochester, VT: Inner Traditions, 1979.

The Story of Christian Music: From Gregorian Chant to Black Gospel. Andrew Wilson-Dickson. Minneapolis, MN: First Fortress Press, 2003.

The Third Ear: On Listening To The World. Joachim-Ernst Berendt. Longmead, Great Britain: Element Books Ltd., 1988.

A Woman's Journey to God. Joan Borysenko, Ph.D. New York, NY: Riverhead Books, 2001.

For more information on Don Campbell's books and CDs as well as a vast guide to music, music therapy, education, and health:

The Mozart Effect Resource Center
P.O. Box 800
Boulder, CO 80306
800-721-2177
www.mozarteffect.com

For more information on Sound Circle, visit their Website: **SoundCircleSing.org**.

Suggested
LISTENING

Ancient & Modern. Anne Dudley. Angel. 7243 5 56868 2 4

Adiemus—Songs of Sanctuary. Virgin. CDVE 925

Deep Listening. Pauline Oliveros. New Albion Records NA022

Floating World. Riley Lee & Marshall McGuire. New World. CD603

Handel's Messiah—A Soulful Celebration. Reprise. 9 96980-2

Healing Powers of Tone and Chant. Don Campbell. Quest Books 978-0-8356-8952-6

Hymns Triumphant, Volumes I & II. Arranged and conducted by Lee Holdridge. Performed by The Amen Choir and London's National Philharmonic Orchestra. Sparrow. BWD 2058

Magnum Mysterium I & II—collection of sacred music classics. Celestial Harmonies. 18.35505

Mass in B Minor—Bach. Orchestra of the 18th Century, Conducted by Frans Bruggen. Philips. 426 238-2

Miserere—Arvo Part. The Hilliard Ensemble. ECM New Series 1430

Monk and the Abbess: Music of Hildegard von Bingen and Meredith Monk. Richard Westenburg. Catalyst. 09026-68329-2

Stor Amhran. Noirin Ni Riain. Sounds True Audio. M270D

Acknowledgments

My deepest appreciation goes to Bill Horwedel at Spring Hill Music for his visionary practicality and suggestions. Thanks to Reid Tracy, Jill Kramer, Jessica Kelley, Christy Salinas, and Julie Davison at Hay House for their skillful development of this book. Thanks also to Rabbi Zalman Schachter-Shalomi, Arthur Harvey, Charles Eagle, Kendyl Gibbons, Chloë Goodchild, Marilyn Rossner, Christine Stevens, Sandra Seagal, Mary Green, Ted Karpf, Alice Parker, and Ysaye Barnwell. Special thanks to Sue Coffee and the singing women of Sound Circle in Boulder, Colorado, who have brought their spirit to the music included in this book. My sincere gratitude to Catherine Viel and Dawn Griffin for their editing and proofing.

~~~

About the
AUTHOR

Don Campbell is a recognized authority on the transformative power of music, listening, and The Mozart Effect®. He's a leading lecturer and consultant to health-care organizations, corporations, parenting groups, and schools. He works with audiences of symphony orchestras on how music can affect learning, healing, and other aspects of our lives.

Don is the acoustic and musical director of Aesthetic Audio Systems, an innovative company that provides quality music to health-care facilities. His books have been translated into 20 languages; and he has lectured in more than 25 countries, including South Africa, Brazil, Poland, Ireland, India, Israel, and Japan. He has recently keynoted conferences for Yale University, the Royal Dublin Society, the Society for the Arts in Healthcare, and the International Teachers' Associations in Japan and South America. He presently serves on the board of the American Music Research Center at the University of Colorado.

Don has served on many national boards, including ARTS for People and Duke University Medical School. In 2004, he was honored with the Distinguished Fellow award from the National Expressive Therapy Association. He has also been awarded "Director Emeritus" of the Boulder Philharmonic Orchestra. In Don's unique view, music is not only a rich and rewarding aesthetic experience, but an easily accessible bridge to a more creative, intelligent, healthy, and joy-filled life. His singular mission is to help return music to its central place in the modern world as a resource for growth, development, health, and celebration.

Don is the author of 22 books, including *The Harmony of Health, Creating Inner Harmony, Music: Physician for Times to Come, Rhythms of Learning,* and the 1997 bestseller *The Mozart Effect.* He has also produced 16 albums, including the accompanying music for the Mozart Effect series for adults and children, which dominated the classical Billboard charts in 1998 and 1999.

❧ ⑤ ☙

Following Sound into Silence: Chanting Your Way Beyond Ego into Bliss, by Kailash (Kurt A. Bruder, Ph.D., M.Ed.) (book-with-CD)

Getting in the Gap: Making Conscious Contact with God Through Meditation, by Dr. Wayne W. Dyer (book-with-CD)

Secrets of the Lost Mode of Prayer: The Hidden Power of Beauty, Blessing, Wisdom, and Hurt, by Gregg Braden

Spirit Medicine: Healing in the Sacred Realms, by Hank Wesselman, Ph.D., and Jill Kuykendall, RPT (book-with-CD)

Yoga, Power, and Spirit: Patanjali the Shaman, by Alberto Villoldo, Ph.D.

Your Soul's Compass: What Is Spiritual Guidance? by Joan Borysenko, Ph.D., and Gordon Dveirin, Ed.D.

❦

All of the above are available at your local bookstore, or may be ordered by contacting Hay House (see last page).

❦

We hope you enjoyed this Hay House book. If you'd like to receive a free catalog featuring additional Hay House books and products, or if you'd like information about the Hay Foundation, please contact:

Hay House, Inc.
P.O. Box 5100
Carlsbad, CA 92018-5100

(760) 431-7695 or (800) 654-5126
(760) 431-6948 (fax) or (800) 650-5115 (fax)
www.hayhouse.com® • www.hayfoundation.org

Published and distributed in Australia by: Hay House Australia Pty. Ltd., 18/36 Ralph St., Alexandria NSW 2015 • *Phone:* 612-9669-4299 *Fax:* 612-9669-4144 • www.hayhouse.com.au

Published and distributed in the United Kingdom by: Hay House UK, Ltd., 292B Kensal Rd., London W10 5BE • *Phone:* 44-20-8962-1230 *Fax:* 44-20-8962-1239 • www.hayhouse.co.uk

Published and distributed in the Republic of South Africa by: Hay House SA (Pty), Ltd., P.O. Box 990, Witkoppen 2068 • *Phone/Fax:* 27-11-467-8904 orders@psdprom.co.za • www.hayhouse.co.za

Published in India by: Hay House Publishers India, Muskaan Complex, Plot No. 3, B-2, Vasant Kunj, New Delhi 110 070 • *Phone:* 91-11-4176-1620 *Fax:* 91-11-4176-1630 • www.hayhouse.co.in

Distributed in Canada by: Raincoast, 9050 Shaughnessy St., Vancouver, B.C. V6P 6E5 • *Phone:* (604) 323-7100 • *Fax:* (604) 323-2600 • www.raincoast.com

Tune in to **HayHouseRadio.com®** for the best in inspirational talk radio featuring top Hay House authors! And, sign up via the Hay House USA Website to receive the Hay House online newsletter and stay informed about what's going on with your favorite authors. You'll receive bimonthly announcements about Discounts and Offers, Special Events, Product Highlights, Free Excerpts, Giveaways, and more!
www.hayhouse.com®